Odom Ministries

SUNDAY SCHOOL

David's Life & Psalms
Sunday School Lessons

Dedication

This set of lessons is dedicated to our wonderful children at the Lighthouse of Living Faith Church. I love you all dearly, and I hope you enjoy these lessons. Be more like David, a man after God's own heart. Learn from his mistakes, sings his psalms, and serve God with all your heart.

Love,

Mimsy

Odom Ministries

SUNDAY SCHOOL

David's Life & Psalms
Sunday School Lessons

DAVID, THE SHEPHERD

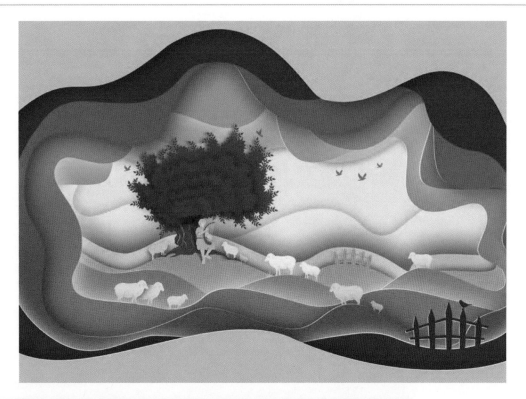

David is a very important person in the Bible. He is the youngest son of a man named "Jesse." He is from the city of Bethlehem (which is a very important city because Jesus was born there). David was a shepherd boy. He took care of his father's sheep. Taking care of sheep is not as easy as it sounds. There were many dangers in the hills surrounding Bethlehem.   David had to protect his father's sheep from dangers in the desert.   The Bible tells us David killed both a bear and a lion when they came after his father's sheep (1 Samuel 17:34-36). David may have been the youngest son of Jesse, but that did not mean his job in the family was unimportant. His father

Did you know sheep are mentioned in the Bible over 500 times? God makes reference to his people, the Israelites, as being sheep.

Abel was the first shepherd mentioned in the Bible.

Jesus is called the "Lamb of God."

relied on David to keep their flocks safe. While we are told in the Bible David was young, he was blessed by God. David knew God was with him in the shepherd's field. David writes some of his most famous psalms while he is a shepherd. One of the most famous is known as the 23rd Psalm. The psalm talks about God as being like a shepherd. Jesus tells us in John 10:11: "I am the Good Shepherd: The Good Shepherd gives his life for his sheep." Since David risked his life for his sheep, we can determine he must have been a good shepherd. As David spent many nights in the shepherd's field and on hillsides taking care of his sheep, God was able to show David how important a shepherd is and how important David was to God. Yes, being a sheep may seem a bit dangerous or frightful at times. But as long as God is our shepherd, we do not have to be afraid. The great thing about God is he looks at each of us and sees our potential. When others looked at

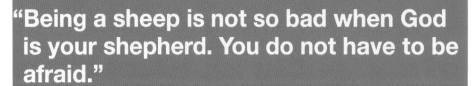

"Being a sheep is not so bad when God is your shepherd. You do not have to be afraid."

-SARAH B. ODOM, PHD

David, they only saw a boy. When God looked at David, he saw a shepherd, warrior, and a king. Trust the Good Shepherd in your life.

Did you know sheep know the voice of their shepherd? In countries where sheep graze in open fields or hillsides, it is important they know their shepherd's voice.

Jesus said this: My sheep hear my voice, and I know them, and they follow me.

We all need to know the voice of Jesus. How do we know his voice? Read his WORD! He speaks to us through the Bible.

Bible References to Shepherds

Biblical Reference	Book/Chapter/Verse
Abel kept sheep, and his sheep sacrifice was pleasing to God.	Genesis 4:2
Abraham had many sheep and gave some away to Abimelech for a treaty with each other.	Genesis 21:27
Moses tended his father-in-law's sheep in the wilderness for years.	Exodus 3:1
David tended his father's sheep in the hills and protected them from danger, like the bear and lion.	1 Samuel 17:34-47
Shepherds were watching sheep in the fields the night Jesus was born.	Luke 2:8
Jesus is the good shepherd.	John 10: 11-15
Jesus wanted Peter to feed his Sheep.	John 21:17

The Good Shepherd

```
L  I  A  S  M  T  H  S  S  G
R  I  E  H  G  O  O  H  I  I
D  O  F  E  S  D  H  E  H  V
E  A  F  E  P  O  H  P  E  E
M  R  E  P  D  O  T  H  H  T
E  H  G  O  O  G  D  E  S  H
T  H  E  P  H  E  R  R  D  G
I  V  E  T  H  H  I  D  S  L
I  F  E  F  O  R  T  H  E  S
H  E  E  P  Q  U  I  F  W  K
```

am	for	giveth
good	his	life
sheep	shepherd	the

_ __ ___ ____ _____ :

___ ____ _____ _____ _

This puzzle is a word search puzzle that has a hidden message in it.

First find all the words in the list.

Words can go in any direction and share letters as well as cross over each other.

Once you find all the words. Copy the unused letters starting in the top left corner into the blanks to reveal the hidden message.

MEMORY CHAPTER: PSALM 23

THE LORD IS MY SHEPHERD; I SHALL NOT WANT.
HE MAKETH ME TO LIE DOWN IN GREEN PASTURES:
HE LEADETH ME BESIDE THE STILL WATERS.
HE RESTORETH MY SOUL:
HE LEADETH ME IN THE PATHS OF RIGHTEOUSNESS
FOR HIS NAME'S SAKE.
YEA, THOUGH I WALK THROUGH THE VALLEY OF THE
SHADOW OF DEATH,
I WILL FEAR NO EVIL: FOR THOU ART WITH ME;
THY ROD AND THY STAFF THEY COMFORT ME.
THOU PREPAREST A TABLE BEFORE ME IN THE
PRESENCE OF MINE ENEMIES:
THOU ANOINTEST MY HEAD WITH OIL; MY CUP
RUNNETH OVER.
SURELY GOODNESS AND MERCY SHALL FOLLOW ME
ALL THE DAYS OF MY LIFE:
AND I WILL DWELL IN THE HOUSE OF THE LORD FOR
EVER.

Psalms 23

When we look at David's Psalm 23, there are several things we notice about his Lord. David tells us how he feels about God as a shepherd. This was something David knew since he was a shepherd.

Questions:

1. How do we know from the verses that God will take care of David?

2. Why does David not fear the valley of the shadow of death?

3. Where does David say he will dwell forever?

FIND MY SHEEP GAME

Find my sheep:

The shepherd stands in the middle of the circle of sheep. The teacher walks around the sheep circle and pats each sheep on the back. On the back of one sheep, the teacher places a sticker. The shepherd will guess who has the sticker. That sheep will turn around to let the shepherd look to see if he/she has the sticker. If the sheep does not have the sticker, the shepherd keep looking for the sheep with the sticker. When the sheep with the sticker is found, that sheep becomes the shepherd. The old shepherd becomes a sheep. The teacher can continue to place a sticker on different children as time allows.

FEED MY SHEEP

Lost Things Cupcakes

1. Either bake cupcakes ahead of time or bake with kids if you have time.
2. Before frosting, placed a small piece of small soft chips, candy, chewy candy in the center of the cupcake.
3. Frost the cupcake.
4. Have students place in small boxes or in bags.
5. Wrap or decorate boxes.
6. Give to someone in church, family, or community.
7. Add your own note to them.

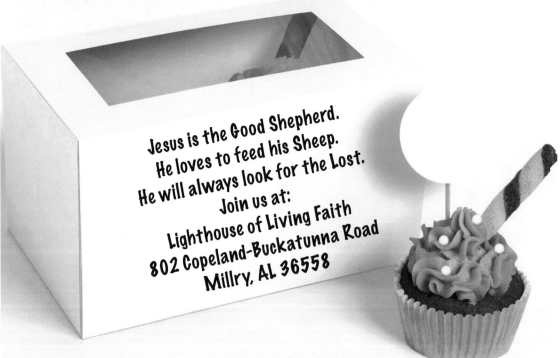

Jesus is the Good Shepherd.
He loves to feed his Sheep.
He will always look for the Lost.
Join us at:
Lighthouse of Living Faith
802 Copeland-Buckatunna Road
Millry, AL 36558

WEEKLY PLAN TO FEED JESUS' SHEEP

This week I will find sheep to feed for Jesus. Each day I will try to do something kind for someone.

1. _____
2. _____
3. _____
4. _____
5. _____
6. _____

DAVID, THE GIANT KILLER

David was more than a shepherd. He was a great warrior. During his life, Israelites (his people and God's people) were struggling to survive. They had their first king (King Saul), and the Philistine army was invading their territory and fighting them. Saul was also a great warrior, but when the Philistine giant, Goliath, challenged the army of God to a warrior-to-warrior winner take all challenge, all of the Israelite army, including Saul, were afraid. Saul did not know what he was going to do. Goliath was mocking the Israelites for their fear of him, and he was mocking their

Goliath was definitely a bully. He tried to bully the Israelites into slavery and servitude by taunting one of them to fight him. Goliath felt no one could defeat him.

The devil is also a bully. He makes us feel like we are small and weak.

Just like David, we need to put our trust in Jesus.

God. Day-after-day this happened, until David came to bring his brothers supplies from his father. David heard Goliath mocking the Israelites and God. He wanted to do something. David wanted to fight the giant. Goliath was anywhere between 9 and 11 feet tall based on the "cubit" size mentioned in the Bible. He was truly a giant. He had protection all around him. It would have seemed impossible for anyone or anything to have enough force to penetrate his armor. However, David had no armor. Saul tried to put his armor on David, but it was too heavy and large for him. So David went with what he knew he could use for a defense. He took his trusted sling and some stones from the nearby brook. David

"David did not need armor when he had God holding his arm!"

-SARAH B. ODOM, PHD

used something familiar to him, his sling, to send the stone through the air. Then it struck its mark. The stone went into the head of the giant. The giant fell quickly. David ran quickly and took the giant's own sword. David killed the giant with it. The Israelites ran to go to battle with the Philistines. The Philistines fled because their warrior was dead. If you resist the devil and all his minions, he will flee away from you too. God will be right there with you when you face your Goliath. Never doubt him.

God doesn't want us to put on someone else's armor. He gives us the armor we need to fight our enemy - the devil.

When we have courage to face our giants in life, we give other people courage.

Always trust God when you have a bully or giant in your life. God will help you; and you can help others.

Goliath is no match for God.

2

Bible Account of David and Goliath

Biblical Reference	Book/Chapter/Verse
David came to see his brothers and bring them corn, cheese and bread.	1 Samuel 17:17
Goliath came out, and all the men of Israel fled from his face in fear.	1 Samuel 17: 23-24
David asked what would be done for the man who killed the giant.	1 Samuel 17: 26
David's brothers were angry with him and thought he was only there to spy on them.	1 Samuel 17: 28
Saul heard about all the words David had said and called for him.	1 Samuel 17: 31
David went to fight the giant for Israel.	1 Samuel 17: 40
David kills Goliath using a sling, stones, and then Goliath's own sword.	1 Samuel 17: 48-51

David's Secret Weapon

A	B	C	D	E	F	G	H	I	J	K	L	M	N	O	P	Q	R	S	T	U	V	W	X	Y	Z
1			13	21			3						23				25								

David's Victory

When we look at David's victory with Goliath, not everything was all good. Sure the people loved him, but David did face those who did not. 1 Samuel 17 and 18 will help you.

Questions:

1. Why do you think David's brothers were angry with him for coming and talking about Goliath?

2. How do the people respond to David killing Goliath?

3. What happens to Saul after he sees how the people respond to David?

The people sang the praises of David for killing their enemy.   1 Samuel 18: 6-7

MEMORY VERSES

**The Lord is my rock,
and my fortress,
and my deliverer;
The God of my rock;
in him will I trust:
he is my shield,
and the horn of my salvation,
my high tower,
and my refuge,
my saviour;
(2 Samuel 22:2 &3)**

SLAY THE GIANT GAME

Slay the Giant:

Materials Needed:
Giant printed out on paper
Paper balls or large Marshmallows
Balloons
Plastic Cups

Instructions:

Students can color or make giant and tape the paper together so the giant stands tall.
Students will make sling with plastic cup and balloon.
Cut out bottom of cup; Tie knot on the end of balloon; cut off end of cup.
Students will hold cup up and pull back on balloon.
Release balloon and paper or marshmallow should shoot out. Try to knock down the giant.

OUTREACH ACTIVITY

Give students an opportunity to paint rocks. You can purchase a little pouch to put them in. Have them give them to members of the church, the elderly, or someone they know who needs a life lift. The stones can have sayings like: Peace, Joy, Faith, Love, Jesus, etc.

Allow them to think of their own message.

Materials needed: stones, pouches, paint or paint markers, brushes.

Make sure to add your church address on a card and put it in the pouch with the stones.

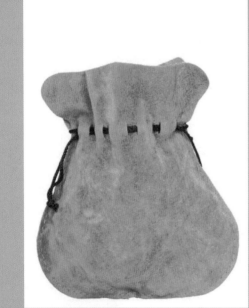

Sample Note:

God always fights for his people.

Remember these little stones.

Lighthouse of Living Faith

802 Copeland Buckatunna Road

Millry, AL 36558

MY WEEKLY PLAN TO REMEMBER GOD

This week I will remember how God fights for me:

_____

_____

_____

_____

_____

_____

_____

_____

_____

Each stone can represent something you remember God has done for you in the past.   Remember to share what you learned with your family and friends.

DAVID RUNS FOR HIS LIFE

David was now a national hero. He had killed the giant, Goliath. At first King Saul was okay with David, even calling David to play his harp to soothe King Saul's mind. But eventually King Saul sets out to kill David. At one point King Saul throws a spear at David and almost hits him. David has to run from King Saul. Even though King Saul seemed to hate David, David had friends in King Saul's family. First of all, David was married to one of King Saul's daughters, Michal. King Saul had allowed David to marry her for killing many Philistines in battle (200 men). King

Music soothes the soul. Godly music can definitely help you feel better.

King Saul loved to hear David play his harp and sing for him. It made the evil thoughts in his heart go away.

When you are sad, listen to Christian music to soothe your heart.

Saul also had a son, Jonathan, who was very good friends with David. Jonathan helped David escape from his father, King Saul. They had a time when David wanted to come home and needed to know if he could. Jonathan told David he would talk to his father. Jonathan would give David a signal to let him know the status of his possible return to the palace. If Jonathan shot the arrows close, David could come home safely. If Jonathan shot the arrows far away, David would know that it was not safe for him to come home. Jonathan had to shoot the arrows far away. This made both Jonathan and David very

"David had a great friend, Jonathan! David had a great enemy, King Saul. Some people love you! Some people do not! "

-SARAH B. ODOM, PHD

sad. King Saul hunted and tried to kill David several times. David even got so close that he cut off part of King Saul's robe and stole his spear. But David would not kill King Saul because he feared the Lord. David knew God had anointed King Saul, and he would not touch God's anointed. David continued to run and build his army until God allowed King Saul to be killed in another battle. God was faithful to David.

Even though Michal and Jonathan loved David, their father hated him.

Be careful to judge all members of a family by one member.

David never forgot what Jonathan did for him, and later he remembered Jonathan's son, Mephibosheth, who had been crippled in the battle that killed Jonathan when his nurse dropped him running for their lives. David brought him to the palace to live.

Bible Account of David On the Run

Biblical Reference	Book/Chapter/Verse
Saul took David to the palace to live with them	1 Samuel 18
Jonathan and David make a covenant with each other to always be friends.	1 Samuel 18
Women of the Israelites sang songs about David, and Saul began to hate him.	1 Samuel 18
Saul threw a javelin (light spear) at David, and David had to flee from him.	1 Samuel 18
Jonathan talked to his father for David, and Saul stopped for a while.	1 Samuel 19
Michal had to help David escape from her father using a window and dummy to look like David in bed.	1 Samuel 19
Jonathan uses arrows to let David know he must not return ever to the palace as long as King Saul lived.	1 Samuel 20

David on the Run

```
R  L  L  M  L  W  J  B  F  J  E  F  I  W  K
T  N  A  U  K  A  I  R  E  O  R  Q  S  J  T
M  X  A  H  V  O  I  A  Y  N  X  F  M  D  Z
H  S  B  E  C  E  Y  R  H  A  R  P  B  P  F
Q  C  L  F  N  I  L  R  A  T  U  L  I  D  U
D  I  Y  D  X  K  M  O  P  H  V  I  K  C  C
N  A  S  Q  S  N  F  W  Z  A  K  K  X  B  Z
P  C  V  F  X  W  V  S  G  N  M  T  R  C  X
K  R  R  I  N  T  D  O  Q  K  W  Z  G  B  E
C  A  D  B  D  A  R  Q  X  Q  F  E  N  J  M
W  D  F  A  A  G  Q  W  G  T  N  P  I  B  T
R  A  E  P  S  T  X  T  B  D  W  X  K  R  J
P  G  H  O  B  P  T  J  S  S  X  W  U  O  E
C  T  T  A  J  H  W  L  F  E  Z  Q  R  F  E
C  C  X  D  S  K  R  B  E  Y  A  Y  D  E  L
```

Arrows	Battle	David
Friends	Harp	Javelin
Jonathan	King	Michal
Saul	Spear	Wife

Find the word in the puzzle.

Words can go in any direction.
Words can share letters as they cross over each other.

David On The Run

David's Story Continues in 1 Samuel 18-20. In these chapters you will find that David must flee for his life. King Saul has turned against him.

Questions:

1. Why do you think King Saul turned against the little shepherd boy who saved Israel?

2. David has at least two opportunities to kill King Saul, but he doesn't. What does this say about David?

3. Jonathan, King Saul's son, continues to be David's friend even though his father even tries to kill Jonathan. What does this say about him?

MEMORY VERSE

And Jonathan said to David,
Go in peace,
forasmuch as we have sworn
both of us in the name of
the Lord, saying,
The Lord be between me
and thee,
and between my seed and thy
seed for ever.
(1 Samuel 20:42)

BE A GOOD FRIEND GAME

Be a Good Friend	Instructions:
Materials Needed:	Students can decorate their Pringles can like a quiver for their arrows. They can then make arrows that have words like: Friend, Kindness, Love, etc.
Pringles Box	
Construction Paper	**Game:**
Markers or Crayons	Students can play a game of "Catch a Friend." One person is Jonathan, others are David. As Jonathan "catches" David, he takes his arrows. Jonathan and "Catch" continues. Jonathan keeps trying to catch the "Davids" with arrows. Last David with Arrows wins.
Twine or Yarn	

OUTREACH ACTIVITY

Materials Needed:

Envelopes

Paper or Blank Cards

Stickers

Cutouts

Markers

Glue or Tape

Stamps

Instructions:

Have students bring an address of a friend to SS or Kids' Church.

Have students create a "Friendship" Card for someone they know.
It could be a family member or friend.

Help students prepare the card and make sure it is stamped.

Remember larger cards may require additional stamps.

Tell students you will mail the cards for them this week.

Have them followup with their friends to see if they got the card.

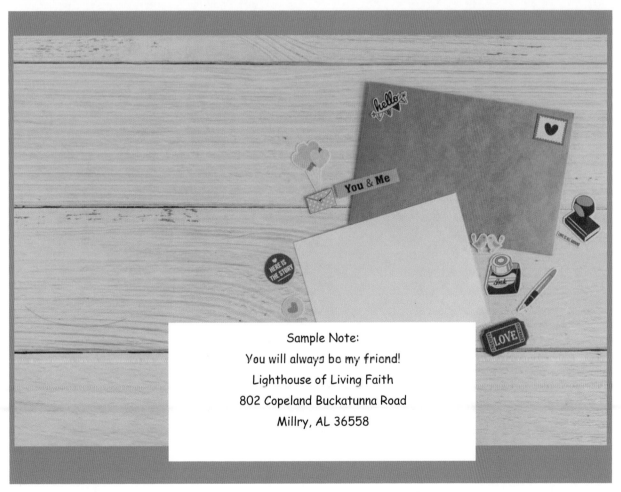

Sample Note:

You will always be my friend!

Lighthouse of Living Faith

802 Copeland Buckatunna Road

Millry, AL 36558

MY WEEKLY PLAN TO BE A FRIEND

This week I will remember to be a good friend:

_____

_____

_____

_____

_____

_____

_____

_____

_____

Each arrow can represent something you do to show you are a good friend to someone. Remember family members can be friends too. But also try to do something for a new friend.

DAVID THE KING

King Saul and Jonathan were killed in battle. When David heard this, he was very sad. He mourned the death of his friend and his King, even though Saul had tried to kill David several times.   At that time Israel was split into two kingdoms (Israel and Judah). Israel appointed Saul's son, Ishbosheth as their king.   Judah anointed David as their king.   Long before the prophet Samuel died, he had anointed David to be the future king of Israel, so it was only a matter of time.   David was 30 years old when he became king over all of Israel. He would have many battles

David began his reign after King Saul's death and the death of his best friend, Jonathan.

David was a young man, and he had to take over a very large kingdom. This was difficult, and David would make mistakes.

David proved to be a King after God's heart. He was a good king.

to fight, and there would be many challenges in David's life. But David was a man after God's heart. David did wrong in his life. He was not perfect. He stole another man's wife, and because he was king, David thought he would get away with it. But God sent another prophet, Nathan, to let David know God knew exactly what David and Bathsheba had done. David had many sorrows in his family after his sin with Bathsheba. But God forgave David because David was truly sorry for his sin. King Saul never really was sorry for the

wrongs he did. He only made excuses. But when Nathan confronted David about his sin, David was sorry. David knew he had done wrong. He asked Nathan to plead with God to forgive him. He would accept God's punishment. The Bible tells us even though David was not a perfect man, he was a good king. Before David died, he gave these words to his son, Solomon: "I go the way of all the earth: be thou strong therefore, and shew thyself a man; And keep the charge of the Lord thy God, to walk in his ways, to keep his statutes, and his commandments, and his judgments, and his testimonies, as it is written in the law of Moses, that thou mayest prosper in all that thou doest, and whithersoever thou turnest thyself." David knew the key to success in life: Walk in God's ways.

Even though David was a good king, he was not a perfect king. David made mistakes that caused him much sorrow.

I believe if King David could tell us anything in person today, he would tell us to always follow God's laws. He told his son, Solomon, this right before David died.

Following God with all our hearts will always give us peace.

Bible Account of King David's Reign

Biblical Reference	Book/Chapter/Verse
David was 30 years old when he began to reign as king.	2 Samuel 5
David brings the Ark of the Covenant back to Jerusalem	2 Samuel 6
David sins with Bathsheba and brings God's judgment on him.	2 Samuel 11
David's son, Solomon, is born. He will follow David as king one day.	2 Samuel 12
David's son, Absalom, rebels against David and is killed.	2 Samuel 15-18
David gives Solomon instructions before he dies.	1 Kings 2
David dies 40 years after he starts his reign as king.	1 Kings 2

David Becomes King

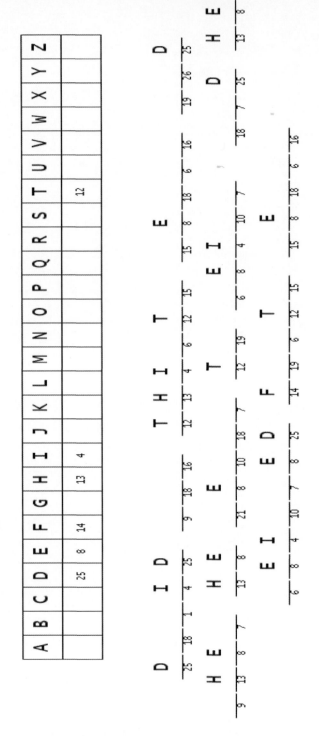

Decode the message.

Each letter in the phrase has been replaced with a random letter or number.

Try to decode the message.

David as King

2 Samuel and 1 Kings give a detailed account of David's reign. David was a good king, but not a perfect king.

Questions:

1. David sinned against God, but repented. Although he had to deal with the consequences, God blessed him. What was the difference between David and Saul?

2. David had a son, Absalom, who rebelled against him. How would this remind David of what he had done to God?

3. David gave his son, Solomon, words to live by after he died. What did David tell Solomon he should do?

MEMORY VERSE

And David went on,
and grew great,
and the Lord God of
hosts was with him.
2 Samuel 5:10

TOSSING THE CROWN

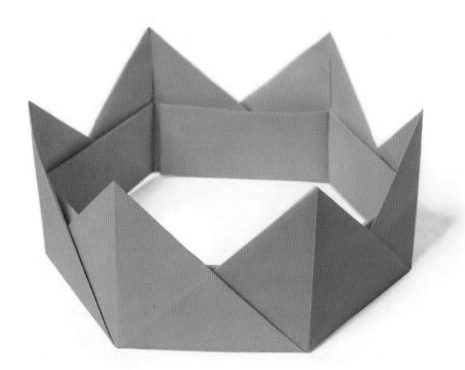

Making the Crown

Google directions for an origami crown.

Show students YouTube videos on how to make them. There are several.

Materials needed:

Cardstock colored paper.

Game: Tossing the Crown

Students can play a game of "Toss the Crown" similar to a ring toss or horse shoes. The student who rings it the most or closest out of 3 tries is the king/queen. You will need a pole or stand for the toss.

OUTREACH ACTIVITY

Materials Needed:

RC Colas (Bottle or Can)
Golden Nugget Candy, any brand, but Hershey's is some of the best.

Instructions:

Have students create goodie bags with the RC Cola and golden nuggets.

Decorate the bags and include a note. It can be a sticky label or just a note put in the bag.

The idea is for children to think of the kindness King David showed to Mephibosheth, Jonathan's son. Tell them to think of someone who might need to be reminded they are royalty. It could be an elderly person, someone who is sick or going through loss, or even a friend or a new student at school. The main thing for them to think of is being like King David and showing kindness.

Sample Note:
You are Royalty to the King of Kings!
Lighthouse of Living Faith
802 Copeland Buckatunna Road
Millry, AL 36558

MY WEEKLY PLAN TO WORK FOR MY KING

This week I will remember to work for my King, Jesus:

_____

_____

_____

_____

_____

_____

_____

_____

_____

_____

Each crown can represent something you do this week to show you are a servant of Jesus Christ. Think of others you can serve. Have fun with your service.

DAVID, THE PSALMIST

David is called the Psalmist.   Many of the psalms found in the Book of Psalms in the Bible are said to be those David wrote.   David is given credit for writing at least 73 of the 150 Psalms.   Some believe he wrote 75. Let's look at the word "psalm".   It means sacred poem or song.   There are at least seven (7) types of psalms found in the Book of Psalms. We will take a look at each kind.   (1) Psalms of Praise - We sing psalms of praise to God to let him know we love him and worship him.   (2) Psalms of Lament - Lament means to be sad or sorry.   We sing psalms of lament when we know we have done something wrong or others

David had many events in his life that helped him have words for his psalms.

We, too, can write psalms to Jesus. We can tell him all about our lives and our trust in him.

There are many famous hymns written by people who loved God.

have done something wrong. (3) Psalms of Thanksgiving - We sing psalms of thanksgiving when we are thankful for what God has done, and we want to let him know we are thankful from our heart and soul. (4) Psalms of Confidence - When we know we can trust in God and he is our King of Kings, we can sing psalms of confidence in him. (5) Psalms of Kingship - We sing these to let God know we believe he is the King of Kings, and we are grateful for all he does for us in his Kingdom. (6) Psalms of Remembrance - We sing these psalms

"Psalms are the best to read when you are happy, sad, upset, or just need to feel close to God."

-SARAH B. ODOM, PHD

when we want God to know we remember all he has done for us. (7) Psalms of Wisdom - We read these psalms to give us guidance. They show us how to live. David is not the only psalmist in the Book of Psalms. Others include Moses, Asaph, the sons of Korah, and Solomon. Psalms was the songbook for the ancient Jewish people. They used it to sing in their tabernacle, and later their temple. They also knew the psalms and sang or read them in their every day lives, such as in the fields while tending their sheep.

David wrote some psalms as though he were talking directly to God.

Hear, O Lord, when I cry with my voice: have mercy also upon me, and answer me. Psalm 27:7

Some of the Psalms were written as if God was speaking to man.

Hear, O my people, and I will speak; O Israel, and I will testify against thee: I am God, even thy God. Psalm 50:7

Top 10 Psalms According to Survey among Readers

Top 10 Psalms	Book/Chapter
The LORD is my shepherd. I shall not want.	Psalm 23
I lift up my eyes to the hills; my help comes from the LORD.	Psalm 121
I give you thanks, O LORD! All the kings of the earth will praise you.	Psalm 138
My soul waits for God alone. He alone is my rock and my salvation.	Psalm 62
God is our refuge. We will not fear, though the earth give way.	Psalm 46
Praise the LORD! For great is his love towards us.	Psalm 117
Do not be envious of evildoers, for they will fade like the grass.	Psalm 37
Blessed is the man who does not walk with the wicked, whose delight is in the law of the LORD.	Psalm 1
I waited patiently for the LORD. He drew me up from the pit.	Psalm 40
How lovely is your dwelling place, O LORD! A day in your courts is better than a thousand elsewhere.	Psalm 84

Psalm of David

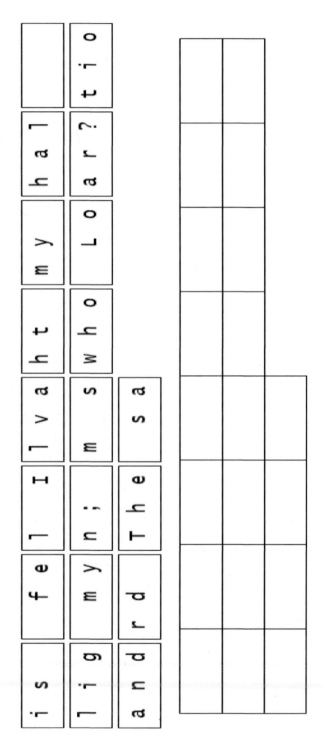

Unscramble the tiles to reveal a message.

Each tile is used only once.

Use spacing, puncuation and common words to find adjacent tiles.

Some words may be split into two lines.

MEMORY SONG FROM PSALMS

BLESS THE LORD, O MY SOUL: AND ALL THAT
IS WITHIN ME, BLESS HIS HOLY NAME.
BLESS THE LORD, O MY SOUL: AND ALL THAT
IS WITHIN ME, BLESS HIS HOLY NAME.
HE HAS DONE GREAT THINGS.
HE HAS DONE GREAT THINGS.
HE HAS DONE GREAT THINGS.
BLESS HIS HOLY NAME.
BLESS THE LORD, O MY SOUL: AND ALL THAT
IS WITHIN ME, BLESS HIS HOLY NAME.
BLESS THE LORD, O MY SOUL: AND ALL THAT
IS WITHIN ME, BLESS HIS HOLY NAME.

Psalms

The Psalms were written so our hearts may be made closer to God. Take a look at a few Psalms below, then decide what each psalm expresses.

Questions:

1. O praise the Lord, all ye nations: praise him, all ye people. For his merciful kindness is great toward us: and the truth of the Lord endureth for ever. Praise ye the Lord. What is this psalm expressing?

2. Blessed is the man that walketh not in the counsel of the ungodly, nor standeth in the way of sinners, nor sitteth in the seat of the scornful. What is this psalm expressing?

3. I have set the Lord always before me: because he is at my right hand, I shall not be moved.Therefore my heart is glad, and my glory rejoiceth: my flesh also shall rest in hope. What is this psalm expressing?

WRITING FROM THE HEART

Writing Psalms (Poems or Songs)
Materials:
Paper, Pen, Pencils, Markers, etc. (Rough paper would be good).
Items from home to help them. It could be a toy, or a book, or a
picture.
Have students think of the type of Psalm they want to write.
(Remember there are 7 types.) Help students come up with a theme.
Have them write their own psalms to read to the class and practice to
read to others. Encourage them to put a tune to them and sing them as
well. Prepare them for a 5th Sunday Evening Psalms Ice Cream Party.

OUTREACH MINISTRY

PSALM 34:8

Taste & See

THAT THE LORD IS GOOD!

Plan a 5th Sunday Ice Cream Party for the whole church to attend.

At the 5th Sunday Party, have kids read their psalms (poems or songs) to the church.

If some kids are too shy, teachers can read or sing their psalms (poems or songs).

Encourage the kids to share with the church what they have learned during their study on David and on Psalms.

SINGING IN MY HEART

This week I will sing in my heart for Jesus. If I am sad, I will lament. If I am happy, I will praise. Either way, I will let God know I love him.

1. _____

2. _____

3. _____

4. _____

5. _____

6. _____

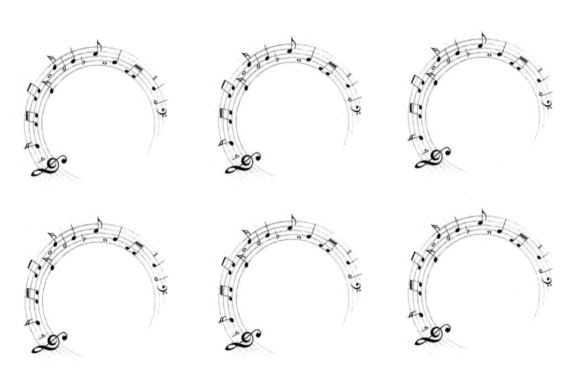

Printed in Great Britain
by Amazon